The Poetry Of Owen Seaman

Owen Seaman was born in Shrewsbury on September 18th, 1861. He was educated at Shrewsbury school and Clare College Cambridge. After graduating he was a school master and then a professor of literature. In 1894 his parody of Kipling 'Rhyme Of The Kipperling' was published in Punch magazine and that same year he published a volume of parodies - 'Horace At Cambridge'. In 1897 he became a barrister at Inner Temple but was invited to join the staff at Punch, which he joined, rising to assistant editor in 1897 and editor in 1906.

In 1914 he was knighted and thereafter his patriotism began to take hold and the following year, 1915, he a published a further book of poetry – 'War Time'.

Never considered an outstanding poet he was none the less much admired. His editorship of Punch was quite remarkable as were several other books of parodies and the such. In 1933, he was created a baronet, of Bouverie Street in the City of London. Sir Owen Seaman, 1st Baronet, never married, and died on February 2nd, 1936 and was buried in Putney Vale Cemetery.

Index Of Contents

The Battle Of The Bays

1. A Song Of Renunication
(AFTER A. C. S.)
In the days of my season of salad,
When the down was as dew on my cheek,
And for French I was bred on the ballad,
For Greek on the writers of Greek,
Then I sang of the rose that is ruddy,
Of 'pleasure that winces and stings,'
Of white women and wine that is bloody,
And similar things.

Of Delight that is dear as Desi-er,
And Desire that is dear as Delight;
Of the fangs of the flame that is fi-er,
Of the bruises of kisses that bite;
Of embraces that clasp and that sever,
Of blushes that flutter and flee
Round the limbs of Dolores, whoever
Dolores may be.

I sang of false faith that is fleeting
As froth of the swallowing seas,
Time's curse that is fatal as Keating
Is fatal to amorous fleas;
Of the wanness of woe that is whelp of
The lust that is blind as a bat
By the help of my Muse and the help of
The relative THAT.

Panatheist, bruiser and breaker
Of kings and the creatures of kings,
I shouted on Freedom to shake her
Feet loose of the fetter that clings;
Far rolling my ravenous red eye,
And lifting a mutinous lid,
To all monarchs and matrons I said I
Would shock them and did.

Thee I sang, and thy loves, O Thalassian,
O 'noble and nude and antique!'
Unashamed in the 'fearless old fashion'
Ere washing was done by the week;
When the 'roses and rapture' that girt you
Were visions of delicate vice,
And the 'lilies and languors of virtue'
Not nearly so nice.

O delights of the time of my teething,
Félise, Fragoletta, Yolande!
Foam-yeast of a youth in its seething
On blasted and blithering sand!
Snake-crowned on your tresses and belted
With blossoms that coil and decay,
Ye are gone; ye are lost; ye are melted
Like ices in May.

Hushed now is the bibulous bubble
Of 'lithe and lascivious' throats;
Long stript and extinct is the stubble
Of hoary and harvested oats;
From the sweets that are sour as the sorrel's
The bees have abortively swarmed;
And Algernon's earlier morals
Are fairly reformed.

I have written a loyal Armada,
And posed in a Jubilee pose;
I have babbled of babies and played a
New tune on the turn of their toes;
Washed white from the stain of Astarte,
My books any virgin may buy;
And I hear I am praised by a party
Called Something Mackay!

When erased are the records, and rotten
The meshes of memory's net;
When the grace that forgives has forgotten
The things that are good to forget;
When the trill of my juvenile trumpet
Is dead and its echoes are dead;
Then the laurel shall lie on the crumpet
And crown of my head!

The Battle Of The Bays

2. For The Albums Of The Crowned Heads Only
(AFTER SIR E. A.)

1. From the third Sa'dine Box of the eighth Gazelle of Ghazal.

Yá Yá! Best-Belovéd! I look to thy dimples and drink;
Tiddlihî! to thy cheek-pits and chin-pit, my Tulip, my Pink!

See my heart rises up like a bubble, and bursts in my throat,
And the dimples that draw it are Three, like the Men in a Boat.

Thrice Three are the Muses, and I that begat her should guess
That the Tenth is the TĒLE-EPHĒMERA, Pride of the PRESS!

And the Graces were triplets till lately the fruitful Dîtî
Propagated a Fourth, and the infant was W. G.

From my post of Propinquity prone on my languorous knees
My tears slither down like the Gum of Arabia's trees.

"Am I drunk?" Heart-Entangler! By Hafiz, the Blender of Squish!
'Tis the camel that sits on the prayer-mat is drunk as a fish.

As I hope for the future Uprising, deny it who can,
Two years I have worn the Blue Ribbon, come next Ramadan!

Chest-Preserver! thou knowest thine eyes, they alone, are my drink,
Blue-black as the sloes of the Garden or Stephens his Ink.

On thy sugar-sweet liplets, my Cypress! I browse like a bee,
And am aching, as after a surfeit of Melon, for thee!

Low laid at thy feet, little feet, in the dust like a worm,
Round the train of thy skirt, O my Peacock, I fitfully squirm.

By Allah! I swoon, I rotate, I am sickly of hue!
And the Infidel swore that Jam-Jam was a Temperance brew!

Heart-Punisher! Surely I think it was jalapped with gin!
Aha! Paradise! I am passing! So be it! Amin!

2. From a little thing by the Princess Onono Goawaī.

The bulbul hummeth like a book
Upon the pooh-pooh tree,
And now and then he takes a look
At you and me,
At me and you.
Kuchi!
Kuchoo!

3. From the Sanskrit of Matabîlîwaijo.

Wind! a word with thee! thou goest where my Well-Preservéd lies
On her bed of bonny briers keeping off the wicked flies.

Thou shalt know her by th' aroma of her bosom, which is musk,
And her ivories that glisten like an elephantine tusk.

Seek her coral-guarded tympanum and whisper "Poppinjai!"
And (referring to her lover) kindly add "A-lal-lal-lai!"

Breeze! thou knowest my condition; state it broadly, if you please,
In a smattering of Indo-Turco-Perso-Japanese.

Say my youth is flitting freely, and before the season goes
From the garden of my Tûtsi I am fain to pluck a rose.

Tell her I'm a wanton Sufí (what a Sufí really is
She may know, perhaps, I count it one of Allah's mysteries).

Fly, O blessed Breeze, and hither bring me back the net result;
Fly as flies the rude mosquito from Abdullah's catapult.

Fly as flies the rusty rickshaw of the Kurumayasan,
When he scents a Hippopotam down the groves of Gulistan.

Fly and cull, O cull, a section of my Pipkin's purple tress;
Thou shalt find me drinking deeply with the Lords that rule the
Mess;

Quaffing mead and mighty sodas with the Johnís, Lords of War,
Talking 'jungle in the gun-room,' underneath the deodar.

Hoo Tawâ! I go to join them; he that cometh late is curst,
For the Lords of War (by Akbar) have a most amazing thirst!

The Battle Of The Bays

3. Marsyas In Hades
(AFTER SIR L. M.)

Next I saw
A pensive gentleman of middle age,
That leaned against a Druid oak, his pipe
Pendent beneath his chin - a double one
(Meaning the pipe); reluctant was his breath,
For he had mingled in the Morris dance
And rested blown; but damsels in their teens,
All decorous and decorously clad,
Their very ankles hardly visible,
Recalled his motions; while, for chaperon,
Good Mrs. Grundy up against the wall
Beamed approbation.

On his face I read
Signs of high sadness such as poets wear,
Being divinely discontented with
The praise of jeunes filles. Even as I looked,
He touched the portion of his pipe reserved
For minor poetry of solemn tone,
Checking the humorous stops intended for
Electioneering posters and the like;
And therewithal he made the following
Addition to his Songs Unsung, or else
His Unremarked Remarks:

"Dear Sir," he said,
"Excuse my saying 'Sir' like that; it is
Our way in Hades here among the damned;
For you must know that some of us are damned
Not only by faint praise but full applause
Of simple critics. Take my case. In me
Behold the good knight Marsyas, M.A.,
Three times a candidate for Parliament,
And twice retired; a Justice of the Peace;
Master of Arts (I said), and better known
In literary spheres as Master of
The Mediocre-Obvious; and read
By boarding-misses in their myriads.
These dote upon me. Sweetly have I sung
The commonplaces of philosophy
In common parlance.

You have read perhaps
The Cymric Triads? Poetry, they say,
Excels alone by sheer simplicity
Of language, subject, and invention. Sir!
The excellence of mine lay that way too.
But fate is partial. Heaven's fulgour moulds
'To happiness some, some to unhappiness!'
(Look you, the harp was Welsh that figured forth
That excellent last line.) I ask you, Sir,
What would you? Ill content with mortal praise,
And haply somewhat overbold, I sought
To be as gods be; sought, in fact, to filch
Apollo's bays!

Ah me! Dear me! I fain
Would use a stronger phrase, but hardly dare,
Being, whatever else, respectable.
I say I tired of vulgar homage, gift
Of ignorance. 'High failure overleaps
The bounds of low successes' (there, again,
The harp that twanged was Welsh, but with an echo
Of Browning). Godlike it must be, I thought,

To climb the giddy brink; to pen, for instance,
An Ode to the Imperial Institute,
And fall, if bound to, from a decent height.

I did and missed the laurel; still I go
On writing; what you hear just now is blank,
Distinctly blank, and might be measured by
The kilomètre; yet I rhyme as well
A little; but it takes a lot of time,
And checks the lapse of my pellucid stream
Not all conveniently."

Thereat he paused,
And wrung the moisture from his pipe; but I,
As one that was intolerably bored,
Took even this occasion to be gone;
And, going, marked him how he took his stile,
Polished the waxen tablets, and began
To make a Royal Pæan by request,
Or so he said.

The Battle Of The Bays

4. The Rhyme Of The Kipperling
(AFTER R. K.)

[N.B. No nautical terms or statements guaranteed.]

Away by the haunts of the Yang-tse-boo,
Where the Yuletide runs cold gin,
And the rollicking sign of the Lord Knows Who
Sees mariners drink like sin;
Where the Jolly Roger tips his quart
To the luck of the Union Jack;
And some are screwed on the foreign port,
And some on the starboard tack;
Ever they tell the tale anew
Of the chase for the kipperling swag;
How the smack Tommy This and the smack Tommy That
They broached each other like a whiskey-vat,
And the Fuzzy-Wuz took the bag.

Now this is the law of the herring fleet that harries the northern main,
Tattooed in scars on the chests of the tars with a brand like the brand of Cain:
That none may woo the sea-born shrew save such as pay their way
With a kipperling netted at noon of night and cured ere the crack of day.

It was the woman Sal o' the Dune, and the men were three to one,
Bill the Skipper and Ned the Nipper and Sam that was Son of a Gun;
Bill was a Skipper and Ned was a Nipper and Sam was the Son of a Gun,
And the woman was Sal o' the Dune, as I said, and the men were three to one.

There was never a light in the sky that night of the soft midsummer gales,
But the great man-bloaters snorted low, and the young 'uns sang like whales;
And out laughed Sal (like a dog-toothed wheel was the laugh that Sal
laughed she):
"Now who's for a bride on the shady side of up'ards of forty-three?"

And Neddy he swore by butt and bend, and Billy by bend and bitt,
And nautical names that no man frames but your amateur nautical wit;
And Sam said, "Shiver my topping-lifts and scuttle my foc's'le yarn,
And may I be curst, if I'm not in first with a kipperling slued astarn!"

Now the smack Tommy This and the smack Tommy That and the
Fuzzy-Wuz smack, all three,
Their captains bold, they were Bill and Ned and Sam respectivelee.

And it's writ in the rules that the primary schools of kippers should get off cheap
For a two mile reach off Foulness beach when the July tide's at neap;
And the lawless lubbers that lust for loot and filch the yearling stock
They get smart raps from the coastguard chaps with their blunderbuss fixed
half-cock.

Now Bill the Skipper and Ned the Nipper could tell green cheese from blue,
And Bill knew a trick and Ned knew a trick, but Sam knew a trick worth two.

So Bill he sneaks a corporal's breeks and a belt of pipeclayed hide,
And splices them on to the jibsail-boom like a troopship on the tide.

And likewise Ned to his masthead he runs a rag of the Queen's,
With a rusty sword and a moke on board to bray like the Horse Marines.

But Sam sniffs gore and he keeps off-shore and he waits for things to stir,
Then he tracks for the deep with a long fog-horn rigged up like a bowchasér.

Now scarce had Ned dropped line and lead when he spots the pipeclayed hide,
And the corporal's breeks on the jibsail-boom like a troopship on the tide;
And Bill likewise, when he ups and spies the slip of a rag of the Queen's,
And the rusty sword, and he sniffs aboard the moke of the Horse Marines.

So they each luffed sail, and they each turned tail, and they
whipped their wheels like mad,
When the one he said "By the Lord, it's Ned!" and the other, "It's
Bill, by Gad!"

Then about and about, and nozzle to snout, they rammed through
breach and brace,
And the splinters flew as they mostly do when a Government test
takes place.

Then up stole Sam with his little ram and the nautical talk flowed free,
And in good bold type might have covered the two front sheets of the P. M. G.

But the fog-horn bluff was safe enough, where all was weed and weft,
And the conger-eels were a-making meals, and the pick of the tackle left
Was a binnacle-lid and a leak in the bilge and the chip of a cracked sheerstrake
And the corporal's belt and the moke's cool pelt and a portrait of Francis Drake.

So Sam he hauls the dead men's trawls and he booms for the harbour-bar,
And the splitten fry are salted dry by the blink of the morning star.

And Sal o' the Dune was wed next moon by the man that paid his way
With a kipperling netted at noon of night and cured ere the crack of day;
For such is the law of the herring fleet that bloats on the northern main,
Tattooed in scars on the chests of the tars with a brand like the brand of Cain.

And still in the haunts of the Yang-tse-boo
Ever they tell the tale anew
Of the chase for the kipperling swag;
How the smack Tommy This and the smack Tommy That
They broached each other like a whiskey-vat,
And the Fuzzy-Wuz took the bag.

The Battle Of The Bays

5. A Ballad Of A Bun
(AFTER J. D.)

'I am sister to the mountains now,
And sister to the sun and moon.'

'Heed not belletrist jargon.'

JOHN DAVIDSON.

From Whitsuntide to Whitsuntide
That is to say, all through the year
Her patient pen was occupied
With songs and tales of pleasant cheer.

But still her talent went to waste
Like flotsam on an open sea;
She never hit the public taste,
Or knew the knack of Bellettrie.

Across the sounding City's fogs
There hurtled round her weary head
The thunder of the rolling logs;
"The Critics' Carnival!" she said.

Immortal prigs took heaven by storm,
Prigs scattered largesses of praise;
The work of both was rather warm;
"This is," she said, "the thing that pays!"

Sharp envy turned her wine to blood
I mean it turned her blood to wine;
And this resolve came like a flood
"The cake of knowledge must be mine!

"I am in Eve's predicament
I sha'n't be happy till I've sinned;
Away!" She lightly rose, and sent
Her scruples sailing down the wind.

She did not tear her open breast,
Nor leave behind a track of gore,
But carried flannel next her chest,
And wore the boots she always wore.

Across the sounding City's din
She wandered, looking indiscreet,
And ultimately landed in
The neighbourhood of Regent Street.

She ran against a resolute
Policeman standing like a wall;
She kissed his feet and asked the route
To where they held the Carnival.

Her strange behaviour caused remark;
They said, "Her reason has been lost;"
Beside her eyes the gas was dark,
But that was owing to the frost.

A Decadent was dribbling by;
"Lady," he said, "you seem undone;
You need a panacea; try
This sample of the Bodley bun.

"It is fulfilled of precious spice,
Whereof I give the recipe;
Take common dripping, stew in vice,
And serve with vertu; taste and see!

"And lo! I brand you on the brow
As kin to Nature's lowest germ;
You are sister to the microbe now,
And second-cousin to the worm."

He gave her of his golden store,
Such hunger hovered in her look;
She took the bun, and asked for more,
And went away and wrote a book.

To put the matter shortly, she

Became the topic of the town;
In all the lists of Bellettrie
Her name was regularly down.

"We recognise," the critics wrote,
"Maupassant's verve and Heine's wit;"
Some even made a verbal note
Of Shakespeare being out of it.

The seasons went and came again;
At length the languid Public cried:
"It is a sorry sort of Lane
That hardly ever turns aside.

"We want a little change of air;
On that," they said, "we must insist;
We cannot any longer bear
The seedy sex-impressionist."

Across the sounding City's din
This rumour smote her on the ear:
"The publishers are going in
For songs and tales of pleasant cheer!"

"Alack!" she said, "I lost the art,
And left my womanhood foredone,
When first I trafficked in the mart
All for a mess of Bodley bun.

"I cannot cut my kin at will,
Or jilt the protoplastic germ;
I am sister to the microbe still,
And second-cousin to the worm!"

The Battle Of The Bays

A Vigo Street Eclogue
(AFTER THE SAME)

Mæcenas. John. George. Arthur. Grant. Richard.

MÆCENAS.
What ho! a merry Christmas! Pff!
Sharp blows the frosty blizzard's whff!
Pile on more logs and let them roll,
And pass the humming wassail-bowl!

JOHN.
The wassail-bowl! the wind is snell!
Drinc hael! and warm the poet's pell!

MÆCENAS.
Richard! say something rustic.

RICHARD.
Lo!
The customary mistletoe,
Prehensile on the apple-bough,
Invites the usual kiss.

GEORGE.
And now
Cathartic hellebore should be
A cure for imbecility.

GRANT.
Now holly-berries have begun
To blush for Women That Have Done.

ARTHUR.
The farmer sticks his stuffy goose!

MÆCENAS.
Come, come, you grow a little loose;
That's Michaelmas; you must remember
That Michaelmas is in September!

ARTHUR.
Northward the swallow sweeps his wing.

MÆCENAS.
No, no! the bird arrives in spring!

ARTHUR.
Such knowledge fits the country clown;
We've better things to note in town.
What's Nature's lore compared with women's?

JOHN.
For this enigma go to S-m-ns;
He is the -

ARTHUR.
Yes, I am, I know,
The devil of a Romeo!

JOHN.
Hark! hark! the waits, the precious waits!
Their music beats at Heaven's gates.

MÆCENAS.
What Bodley wight will sing a stave
To match their strumming? I would have

The manly bass of Hobbes's voice;
But Unwin's house is Hobbes's choice.
George! you've a baritone at need.

GEORGE.
Alas! my famous Keynotes lead
To Discords.

JOHN.
I've a little thing
Of Resurrection. Shall I sing?

ARTHUR.
Please do; but à propos of what?

JOHN.
I cannot say, unless de bottes.

[Proceeds to sing a Ballad of Resurrection.

A letter-card from my dear love!
O folded page of blessed blue!
She burst her many-buttoned glove,
And ripped the perforation through.

"My love, to-night, about eleven,
With never a priest or passing-bell,
We die! and meet, with luck, in Heaven,
But anyhow at least in Hell!"

Her courage very nearly failed,
In fact she swooned along the floor;
But curiosity prevailed,
She came again and read some more.

"There is no way but this to choose;
My people fain would have us wed;
But you and I have later views,
And scorn the vulgar marriage-bed.

"Far be it from me to dictate
How best to break the mortal bond,
But personally I may state
That I shall use the village pond.

"Be punctual, love, and let us meet
For weal or woe!
This line has lost a pair of feet;
The post is now about to go."

Ay, ay, she thought, to meet were well,
But if we found each other out?

You, say, in Heaven, I in Hell,
Or else the other way about!

Nay, there be heavy odds, she said,
One fate shall save us both or damn;
We surely shall be bracketed!
She ceased and sent a telegram.

To Guy le Preux de Balthazar
Here followed his address, and then
This pregnant message "Right you are!"
She wrote it with the office pen.

She flashed the phrase along the wires,
Then, passing by a dagger-shop,
Bought one and wiped it on her sire's
Best graduated razor-strop.

On second thoughts, she said, I lean
To poison; true, a knife like this
Looks pretty, rib and rib between,
But people very often miss.

She sought the chemist in his place;
He sampled her with searching eye;
She looked him frankly in the face,
And told a wicked, wicked lie.

"My hen," she said, "a bantam blend
Has hatched a poor demented chick;
To ease the gentle creature's end
I want a pint of arsenic."

The chemist deemed the order large,
But said no thing and drew the drug;
She seized and bore the sacred charge
Before her in a pewter mug.

At tea she faced her fell intent;
Dressing, she lightly laughed at doom;
Dined with the family, and spent
The evening in the drawing-room.

At ten the early rooster crowed;
Ten-thirty struck and she was gone;
She crossed alone the naked road;
The road had really nothing on.

Her golden braids hung down her back;
Within her side she felt a stitch;
And once the moon behind the wrack
Came out and caught her in a ditch.

Once ere she reached the trysting-pear
She broke the slumber of the rooks;
She wrung her hands, she tore her hair,
And did as people do in books.

From out her cloak she fetched the drug
"Thy health, my love, in Heaven or Hell!"
Deep to the dregs she drained the mug
And dropped it, feeling far from well.

Upon the punctual stroke her fond
True lover kept the oath he swore;
Plunged softly in the village pond,
But feeling chilly swam ashore.

Next morning in the judgment-place
Two pallid prisoners were tried;
Their guilt was plain; it was a case
Of ineffective suicide.

Yestreen a member of the Force
Had found a woman deadly sick,
Lamenting, with sincere remorse,
An overdose of arsenic.

Another heard upon his beat
One darkly muttering, "This is Hell!"
His weed was wet from head to feet;
He put him in a common cell.

The Justice chewed the evidence;
His eyes were soft, his lips were bland;
It was, he said, a first offence;
He merely gave a reprimand.

"Go free, my poppets, keep the laws,
And get ye wed at once," said he;
The court indulged in rude applause;
The usher cleared the gallery.

The prison-warder, deeply stirred,
Approached the culprits at the bar;
Then haled them forth without a word
Towards the nearest Registrar.

RICHARD.
John, you surpass yourself. Next week
Expect a flattering critique!

JOHN.
The waits are whining in the cold

With clavicorn and clarigold;
They play them like a crumpled horn,
The clarigold and clavicorn.

The Battle Of The Bays

7. An Ode To Spring In The Metropolis
(AFTER R. LE G.)

Is this the Seine?
And am I altogether wrong
About the brain,
Dreaming I hear the British tongue?
Dear Heaven! what a rhyme!
And yet 'tis all as good
As some that I have fashioned in my time,
Like bud and wood;
And on the other hand you couldn't have a more precise or neater
Metre.

Is this, I ask, the Seine?
And yonder sylvan lane,
Is it the Bois?
Ma foi!
Comme elle est chic, my Paris, my grisette!
Yet may I not forget
That London still remains the missus
Of this Narcissus.

No, no! 'tis not the Seine!
It is the artificial mere
That permeates St. James's Park.
The air is bosom-shaped and clear;
And, Himmel! do I hear the lark,
The good old Shelley-Wordsworth lark?
Even now, I prithee,
Hark
Him hammer
On Heaven's harmonious stithy,
Dew-drunken like my grammar!

And O the trees!
Beneath their shade the hairless coot
Waddles at ease,
Hushing the magic of his gurgling beak;
Or haply in Tree-worship leans his cheek
Against their blind
And hoary rind,
Observing how the sap
Comes humming upwards from the tap-
Root!

Thrice happy, hairless coot!

And O the sun!
See, see, he shakes
His big red hands at me in wanton fun!
A glorious image that! it might be Blake's;
As in my critical capacity I took occasion to remark elsewhere,
When heaping praise
On this exceptionally happy phrase,
Although I made it up myself.
But I and Blake, we really constitute a pair,
Each being rather like an artless woodland elf.

And O the stars! I cannot say
I see a star just now,
Not at this time of day;
But anyhow
The stars are all my brothers;
(This verse is shorter than the others).

O Constitution Hill!
(This verse is shorter still).

Ah! London, London in the Spring!
You are, you know you are,
So full of curious sights,
Especially by nights.
From gilded bar to gilded bar
Youth goes his giddy whirl,
His heart fulfilled of Music-Hall,
His arm fulfilled of girl!
I frankly call
That last effect a perfect pearl!

I know it's
Not given to many poets
To frame so fair a thing
As this of mine, of Spring.
Indeed, the world grows Lilliput
All but
A precious few, the heirs of utter godlihead,
Who wear the yellow flower of blameless bodlihead!

And they, with Laureates dead, look down
On smaller fry unworthy of the crown,
Mere mushroom men, puff-balls that advertise
And bravely think to brush the skies.
Great is advertisement with little men!
Moi, qui vous parle, L- G-ll-nn-,
Have told them so;
I ought to know!

8. Yet
(AFTER F. E. W.)

Sing me a drawing-room song, darling!
Sing by the sunset's glow;
Now while the shadows are long, darling;
Now while the lights are low;
Something so chaste and so coy, darling!
Something that melts the chest;
Milder than even Molloy, darling!
Better than Bingham's best.

Sing me a drawing-room song, darling!
Sing as you sang of yore,
Lisping of love that is strong, darling!
Strong as a big barn-door;
Let the true knight be bold, darling!
Let him arrive too late;
Stick in a bower of gold, darling!
Stick in a golden gate.

Sing me a drawing-room song, darling!
Bear on the angels' wings
Children that know no wrong, darling!
Little cherubic things!
Sing of their sunny hair, darling!
Get them to die in June;
Wake, if you can, on the stair, darling!
Echoes of tiny shoon.

Sing me a drawing-room song, darling!
Sentiment may be false,
Yet it will worry along, darling!
Set to a tum-tum valse;
See that the verses are few, darling!
Keep to the rule of three;
That will be better for you, darling!
Certainly better for me.

9. Elegi Musarum
(AFTER W. W.)

[To Mr. St. Loe Strachey.]

Dawn of the year that emerges, a fine and ebullient Phœnix,
Forth from the cinders of Self, out of the ash of the Past;

Year that discovers my Muse in the thick of purpureal sonnets,
Slating diplomacy's sloth, blushing for 'Abdul the d----d';
Year that in guise of a herald declaring the close of the tourney
Clears the redoubtable lists hot with the Battle of Bays;
Binds on the brows of the Tory, the highly respectable Austin,
Laurels that Phœbus of old wore on the top of his tuft;

Leaving the locks of the hydra, of Bodley the numerous-headed,
Clean as the chin of a boy, bare as a babe in a bath;
Year that I see in the vista the principal verb of the sentence
Loom as a deeply-desired bride that is late at the post
Year that has painfully tickled the lachrymal nerves of the Muses,
Giving Another the gift due to Respectfully Theirs;
Hinc illæ lacrimæ! Ah, reader! I grossly misled you;
See, it was false; there is no principal verb after all!

His likewise is the anguish, who followed with soft serenading
Me as the tremulous tide tracks the meandering moon;
Climbing as Romeo clomb, peradventure by help of a flower-pot,
Where in her balconied bower lay, inexpressibly coy,
Juliet, not as the others, supinely, insanely erotic,
Pallid and yellow of hue, very degenerate souls,
Rioting round with the rapture of palpitant ichorous ardour,
But an immaculate maid, 'one,' you may say, 'of the best'!
His, I repeat, is the anguish, my journalist, eulogist critic,
Strachey, the generous judge, Saintly unlimited Loe!

Vainly the stolid Spectator, bewildered with fabulous bow-wows,
Sick with a surfeit of dog, ran me for all it was worth!
Vainly if I may recur to a metaphor drawn from the ocean,
Long (in a figure of speech) tied to the tail of the moon
Vainly, O excellent organ! with ample and aqueous unction
Once, as a rule, in a week, 'cleansing the Earth of her stain';
(Here you will possibly pardon the natural scion of poets,
Proud with humility's pride, spoiling a passage from Keats)
Vainly your voice on the ears of impregnable Laureate-makers,
Rang as the sinuous sea rings on a petrified coast;
Vainly your voice with a subtle and slightly indelicate largess,
Broke on an obdurate world hymning the advent of Me;
When from the 'commune of air,' from 'the exquisite fabric of Silence,'
I, a superior orb, burst into exquisite print!

What shall we say for your greeting, O good horticultural Alfred!
Royalty's darling and pride, crown of the Salisbury Press?
Now when the negligent Public, in search of a subject for dinner,
Asks for the names of your books, Lord! what a boom there will be!
Hoarse in Penbryn are the howlings that rise for the hope of the Cymri;
Over her Algernon's head Putney composes a dirge;
Edwin anathematises politely in various lingos;
Davidson ruminates hard over a Ballad of Hell;
Fondly Le Gallienne fancies how pretty the Delphian laurels

Would have appeared on his own hairy and passionate poll;
I, imperturbably careless, untainted of jealousy's jaundice,
Simply regret the profane contumely done to the Muse;
Done to the Muse in the person of Me, her patron, that never
Licked Ministerial lips, dusted the boots of the Court!
Surely I hear through the noisy and nauseous clamour of Carlton
Sobs of the sensitive Nine heave upon Helicon's hump!

To Mr. William Watson
[On writing the first instalment of The Purple East, a 'fine sonnet which it is our
privilege to publish.' -Westminster Gazette, Dec. 16, 1895.]

Dear Mr. Watson, we have heard with wonder,
Not all unmingled with a sad regret,
That little penny blast of purple thunder,
You issued in the Westminster Gazette;
The Editor describes it as a sonnet;
I wish to make a few remarks upon it.

Never, O craven England, nevermore
Prate thou of generous effort, righteous aim!
So ran the lines, and left me very sore,
For you may guess my heart was hot with shame:
Even thus early in your ample song
I felt that something must be really wrong.

But when I learned that our ignoble nation
Lay sleeping like a log, and lay alone,
Propping, according to your information,
Abdul the Damned on his infernal throne,
O then I scattered to the wind my fears,
And nearly went and joined the Volunteers.

But just in time the thought occurred to me
That England commonly commits her course
To men as good at heart as even we
And possibly much richer in resource;
That we had better mind our own affairs
And leave these gentlemen to manage theirs.

It further seemed a work uncommon light
For one like you, a casual civilian,
To order half a hemisphere to fight
And slaughter one another by the million,
While you yourself, a paper Galahad,
Spilt ink for blood upon a blotting-pad.

The days are gone when sword and poet's pen
One gallant gifted hand was wont to wield;
When Taillefer in face of Harold's men

Rode foremost on to Senlac's fatal field,
And tossed his sword in air, and sang a spell
Of Roland's battle-song, and, singing, fell.

The days are gone when troubadours by dozens
Polished their steel and joined the stout crusade,
Strumming, in memory of pretty cousins,
The Girl I left behind Me, on parade;
They often used to rattle off a ballad in
The intervals of punishing the Saladin.

In later times, of course I know there's Byron,
Who by his own report could play the man;
I seem to see him with his Lesbian lyre on,
And brandishing a useful yataghan;
Though never going altogether strong, he
Managed at least to die at Missolonghi.

No more the trades of lute and lance are linked,
Though doubtless under many martial bonnets
Brave heads there be that harbour the distinct
Belief that they can manufacture sonnets;
But on the other hand a bard is not
Supposed to run the risk of being shot.

Then since your courage lacks a crucial test,
And politics were never your profession,
Dear Mr. Watson, won't you find it best
To temper valour with a due discretion?
That so, despite the fond Spectator's booming,
Above your brow the bays may yet be blooming.

England's Alfred Abroad

[M. Alfred Austin, poète-lauréat d'Angleterre, vient d'arriver à Nice, où il a
devancé la Reine. Il était, hier, dans les jardins de Monte-Carlo. Sera-ce sous
notre ciel qu'il écrira son premier poème? - Menton-Mondain.]

Wrong? are they wrong? Of course they are,
I venture to reply;
For I bore 'my first' (and, I hope, my worst)
A month or so gone by;
And I can't repeat it under this
Or any other sky.

What! has the public never heard
In these benighted climes
That nascent note of my Laureate throat,
That fluty fitte of rhymes
Which occupied about a half
A column of the Times?

They little know what they have lost,
Nor what a carnal beano
They might have spent in the thick of Lent
If only Daniel Leno
Had sung them Jameson's Ride and knocked
The Monaco Casino.

Some day the croupiers' furtive eyes
Will all be wringing wet;
Even the Prince will hardly mince
The language of regret
At entertaining unawares
The famed Alhambra Pet.

But still not quite incognito
I mark the moving scene,
In a tepid zone where (like my own)
The palms are ever green,
And find myself reported as
A herald of the Queen.

Here where aloft the heavens are blue,
And blue the seas below,
I roll my eye and fondly try
To get the rhymes to go,
As I pace The Garden that I love,
Composing all I know.

But when my poet-pinions droop,
And all the air is wan,
I enter in to the courts of sin
And put a louis on,
And hold my heart and look again,
And lo! the thing is gone!

Wrong? is it wrong? To baser crafts
Has England's Alfred pandered,
Who once to the sign of Phœbus' shrine
With awesome gait meandered,
And ever wrote in the cause of right
According to his Standard?

Nay! this is life! to take a turn
On Fortune's captious crust;
To pluck the day in a human way
Like men of common dust;
But O! if England's only bard
Should absolutely bust!

A laureate never borrows on
His coming quarter's pay;

And I mean to stop or ever I pop
My crown of peerless bay;
So I'll take the next rapide to Nice,
And the 'bus to Cimiez.

MENTONE, Feb., 1896.

Lilith Libifera

Exhumed from out the inner cirque of Hell
By kind permission of the Evil One,
Behold her devilish presentment, done
By Master Aubrey's weird unearthly spell!
This is that Lady known as Jezebel,
Or Lilith, Eden's woman-scorpion,
Libifera, that is, that takes the bun,
Borgia, Vivien, Cussed Damosel.

Hers are the bulging lips that fairly break
The pumpkin's heart; and hers the eyes that shame
The wanton ape that culls the cocoa-nuts.
Even such the yellow-bellied toads that slake
Nocturnally their amorous-ardent flame
In the wan waste of weary water-butts.

Ars Postera
[On an advertisement of A Comedy of Sighs.]

Mr. Aubrey Beer de Beers,
You're getting quite a high renown;
Your Comedy of Leers, you know,
Is posted all about the town;
This sort of stuff I cannot puff,
As Boston says, it makes me 'tired';
Your Japanee-Rossetti girl
Is not a thing to be desired.

Mr. Aubrey Beer de Beers,
New English Art (excuse the chaff)
Is like the Newest Humour style,
It's not a thing at which to laugh;
But all the same, you need not maim
A beauty reared on Nature's rules;
A simple maid au naturel
Is worth a dozen spotted ghouls.

Mr. Aubrey Beer de Beers,
You put strange phantoms on our walls,
If not so daring as To-day's,
Nor quite so Hardy as St. Paul's;
Her sidelong eyes, her giddy guise,

Grande Dame Sans Merci she may be;
But there is that about her throat
Which I myself don't care to see.

Mr. Aubrey Beer de Beers,
The Philistines across the way,
They say her lips - well, never mind
Precisely what it is they say;
But I have heard a drastic word
That scarce is fit for dainty ears;
But then their taste is not the kind
Of taste to flatter Beer de Beers.

Bless me, Aubrey Beer de Beers,
On fair Elysian lawns apart
Burd Helen of the Trojan time
Smiles at the latest mode of Art;
Howe'er it be, it seems to me,
It's not important to be New;
New Art would better Nature's best,
But Nature knows a thing or two.

Aubrey, Aubrey Beer de Beers,
Are there no models at your gate,
Live, shapely, possible and clean?
Or won't they do to 'decorate'?
Then by all means bestrew your scenes
With half the lotuses that blow,
Pothooks and fishing-lines and things,
But let the human woman go!

A New Blue Book
[It was hardly to be supposed that the young decadents who once rioted ... in
the Yellow Book would be content to remain in obscurity after the
metamorphosis of that periodical and the consequent exclusion of themselves.
The Savoy, we learn, to be edited by Mr. Arthur Symons and Mr. Aubrey
Beardsley, will appear early in December. Globe.]

'The world's great age begins anew,'
Cold virtue's weeds are cast;
Our heads are light, our tales are blue,
And things are moving fast;
And no one any longer quarrels
With anybody else's morals.

A racier journal stamps its pages
With Beardsleys braver far;
A bolder Editor engages
To shame the morning star,
On London Nights, not near so chilly,
Sampling a shadier Piccadilly.

Satyr and Faun their late repose
Now burst like anything;
New Mænads, turning sprightlier toes,
Enjoy a jauntier fling;
With lustier lips old Pan shall play
Drain-pipes along the sewer's way.

Priapus, wrongly left for dead,
Is dead no more than Pan;
Silenus rises from his bed
And hiccups like a man;
There's something rather chaste (between us)
About Priapus and Silenus.

O cease to brew your Bodley pap
Whence all the spice is spent!
The splendour of its primal tap
Was gone when Aubrey went;
Behold that subtle Sphinx prepare
Fresh liquors fit to lift your hair.

Another Magazine shall rise
And paint the palsied town,
Of humbler hue, of simpler size,
And sold at half a crown;
Please note the pregnant brand - Savoy,
And don't confuse with saveloy.

To A Boy Poet Of The Decadence
[Showing curious reversal of epigram - 'La nature l'a fait sanglier; la civilisation
l'a réduit à l'état de cochon.']

But my good little man, you have made a mistake
If you really are pleased to suppose
That the Thames is alight with the lyrics you make;
We could all do the same if we chose.

From Solomon down, we may read, as we run,
Of the ways of a man and a maid;
There is nothing that's new to us under the sun,
And certainly not in the shade.

The erotic affairs that you fiddle aloud
Are as vulgar as coin of the mint;
And you merely distinguish yourself from the crowd
By the fact that you put 'em in print.

You're a 'prentice, my boy, in the primitive stage,
And you itch, like a boy, to confess:
When you know a bit more of the arts of the age

You will probably talk a bit less.

For your dull little vices we don't care a fig,
It is this that we deeply deplore;
You were cast for a common or usual pig,
But you play the invincible bore.

To Julia In Shooting Togs
and a Herrickose vein.

Whenas to shoot my Julia goes,
Then, then, (methinks) how bravely shows
That rare arrangement of her clothes!

So shod as when the Huntress Maid
With thumping buskin bruised the glade,
She moveth, making earth afraid.

Against the sting of random chaff
Her leathern gaiters circle half
The arduous crescent of her calf.

Unto th' occasion timely fit,
My love's attire doth show her wit,
And of her legs a little bit.

Sorely it sticketh in my throat,
She having nowhere to bestow't,
To name the absent petticoat.

In lieu whereof a wanton pair
Of knickerbockers she doth wear,
Full windy and with space to spare.

Enlargéd by the bellying breeze,
Lord! how they playfully do ease
The urgent knocking of her knees!

Lengthways curtailéd to her taste
A tunic circumvents her waist,
And soothly it is passing chaste.

Upon her head she hath a gear
Even such as wights of ruddy cheer
Do use in stalking of the deer.

Haply her truant tresses mock
Some coronal of shapelier block,
To wit, the bounding billy-cock.

Withal she hath a loaded gun,

Whereat the pheasants, as they run,
Do make a fair diversión.

For very awe, if so she shoots,
My hair upriseth from the roots,
And lo! I tremble in my boots!

The Links Of Love

My heart is like a driver-club,
That heaves the pellet hard and straight,
That carries every let and rub,
The whole performance really great;
My heart is like a bulger-head,
That whiffles on the wily tee,
Because my love has kindly said
She'll halve the round of life with me.

My heart is also like a cleek,
Resembling most the mashie sort,
That spanks the object, so to speak,
Across the sandy bar to port;
And hers is like a putting-green,
The haven where I boast to be,
For she assures me she is keen
To halve the round of life with me.

Raise me a bunker, if you can,
That beetles o'er a deadly ditch,
Where any but the bogey-man
Is practically bound to pitch;
Plant me beneath a hedge of thorn,
Or up a figurative tree,
What matter, when my love has sworn
To halve the round of life with me?

Swords And Ploughshares
Part I. Presto Furioso

Spontaneous Us!
O my Camarados! I have no delicatesse as a diplomat, but I go blind
on Libertad!
Give me the flap-flap of the soaring Eagle's pinions!
Give me the tail of the British lion tied in a knot inextricable,
not to be solved anyhow!
Give me a standing army (I say 'give me,' because just at present we
want one badly, armies being often useful in time of war).

I see our superb fleet (I take it that we are to have a superb fleet
built almost immediately);
I observe the crews prospectively; they are constituted of various

nationalities, not necessarily American;
I see them sling the slug and chew the plug;
I hear the drum begin to hum;

Both the above rhymes are purely accidental and contrary to my
principles.
We shall wipe the floor of the mill-pond with the scalps of
able-bodied British tars!
I see Professor Edison about to arrange for us a torpedo-hose on
wheels, likewise an infernal electro-semaphore;
I see Henry Irving dead-sick and declining to play Corporal
Brewster;
Cornell, I yell! I yell Cornell!

I note the Manhattan boss leaving his dry-goods store and investing
in a small Gatling-gun and a ten-cent banner;
I further note the Identity evolved out of forty-four spacious and
thoughtful States;
I note Canada as shortly to be merged in that Identity; similarly
Van Diemen's Land, Gibraltar and Stratford-on-Avon;
Briefly, I see Creation whipped!

O ye Colonels! I am with you (I too am a Colonel and on the
pension-list);
I drink to the lot of you; to Colonels Cleveland, Hitt, Vanderbilt,
Chauncey M. Depew, O'Donovan Rossa and the late Colonel
Monroe;
I drink an egg-flip, a morning-caress, an eye-opener, a maiden-bosom,
a vermuth-cocktail, three sherry-cobblers and a gin-sling!
Good old Eagle!

Part II. Intermezzo Doloroso
[Allowing time for the fall of American securities to the extent of some odd
hundred millions sterling; also for the Day of Rest.]

Part III. Andante Amabile
Who breathed a word of war?
Why, surely we are men and Plymouth brothers!
Pray, what in thunder should we cut each other's
Carotids for?

Merciful powers forefend!
For we by gold-edged bonds are bound alway,
Besides a lot of things that never pay
A dividend!

Christmas! we cry thee Ave!
At such a time, when hearts with love are filled,
It seems inopportune for us to build
The needful navy.

In fact in many a church
Uprise the prayer and supplicating psalm
That Heaven would keep our spreading Eagle calm
Upon his perch.

Goodwill and peace and plenty!
Our leading congregations here agree
To vote for this arrangement, nemine
Contradicente.

Greatly be they extolléd
Who occupied the tabernacle-chair
And put it to the meeting then and there
And passed it solid!

That print has also played
A useful part that sent an invitation
To Redmond to relieve the situation
(Answer prepaid).

Say, Sirs, and shall we sever?
And mar the fair exchange of fatted steers,
Chicago pig, and eligible peers?
No! never, never!

Shall gore be made to flow?
Like kindred Sohrabs shall we knock our Rustums,
And blast our beautiful McKinley customs?
Lord love us! no!

Then, burst the sundering bar!
Our punctured pockets yearn across the ocean;
Till now we never had the faintest notion
How dear you are!

O love of other years!
Wall Street, aweary for her broken bliss,
Waits like a loving crocodile to kiss
Again with tears!

To The Lord Of Potsdam
[On sending a certain telegram.]

Majestic Monarch! whom the other gods,
For fear of their immediate removal,
Consulting hourly, seek your awful nod's
Approval;

Lift but your little finger up to strike,
And lo! 'the massy earth is riven' (Shelley),

The habitable globe is shaken like
A jelly.

By your express permission for the last
Eight years the sun has regularly risen;
And editors, that questioned this, have passed
To prison.

In Art you simply have to say, "I shall!"
Beethoven's fame is rendered transitory;
And Titian cloys beside your clever all-
egory.

We hailed you Admiral: your eagle sight
Foresaw Her Majesty's benign intentions;
A uniform was ready of the right
Dimensions.

Your wardrobe shines with all the shapes and shades,
That genius can fix in fancy suitings;
For levées, false alarums, full parades
And shootings.

But save the habit marks the man of gore
Your spurs are yet to win, my callow Kaiser!
Of fighting in the field you know no more
Than I, Sir!

When Grandpapa was thanking God with hymns
For gallant Frenchmen dying in the ditches,
Your nurse had barely braced your little limbs
In breeches.

And doubtless, where he roosts beside his bock,
The Game Old Bird that played the leading fiddle
Smiles grimly as he hears your perky cock-
-a-diddle.

Be well advised, my youthful friend, abjure
These tricks that smack of Cleon and the tanners;
And let the Dutch instruct a German Boor
In manners.

Nor were you meant to solve the nations' knots,
Or be the Earth's Protector, willy-nilly;
You only make yourself and royal Pots-
dam silly.

Our racing yachts are not at present dressed
In bravery of bunting to amuse you,
Nor can the licence of an honoured guest
Excuse you.

But if your words are more than wanton play
And you would like to meet the old sea-rover,
Name any course from Delagoa Bay
To Dover.

Meanwhile observe a proper reticence;
We ask no more; there never was a rumour
Of asking Hohenzollerns for a sense
Of humour!

From The Lord Of Potsdam

We, William, Kaiser, planted on Our throne
By heaven's grace, but chiefly by Our own,
Do deign to speak. Then let the earth be dumb,
And other nations cease their senseless hum!
Seldom, if ever, does a chance arise
For Us to pose before Our people's eyes;
But this is one of them, this natal day
Whereon Our Ancient and Imperial sway,
Which to the battle's death-defying trump
Welded the States in one confounded lump,
(As many tasty meats are blent within
The German sausage's encircling skin)
By Our decree is twenty-five precisely,
And, under Us (and God) still doing nicely.
Therefore ye Princelings, Plenipotentates,
And Representatives of various States,
A cool Imperial pint your Kaiser drains,
Both to Our 'more immediate' domains,
And to Our lands, Our isles beyond the sea,
Our World-embracing Greater Germany!
Let loose the breathings of Our Royal Band,
We give a rouse, hoch! hoch! to HELGOLAND!

[Kaiserliche Kapelle plays: O Helgoland! mein Helgoland! Air - Die Wacht am Rhein.]

WILLIAM, KAISER, continues:
There are that languish on this festal day
Damned and impounded for lèse-majesté;
We, William, in Our plentitude of grace,
Propose to pardon every hundredth case;
And though their sentence was no more than just
We offer each a copy of Our bust,
With option of a fine; but, be it known,
Whoso again shall deem his life his own,
Or find in Ours the faintest flaw or fleck,
God helping, We will hang him by the neck.
Yea, he shall surely curse his impious star
That dares to question Who or where We are!

Worship your Cæsar, and (C.V.) your God;
Who spares the child may haply spoil the rod.
Many Our uniforms, but We are one,
And one Our empire over which the sun,
Careering on his cloud-compulsive way,
Sets once, but never more than once, a day.
The seas are Ours: world-wide upon the oceans
Our fleet commands the liveliest emotions;
Go where you will, you find Our German manners
Prevailing under other people's banners;
Go where you will, you cannot but remark
The cheap, but never nasty, German clerk;
Observe Our exports; do you ever see
Things made as they are made in Germany?
Always at home on Earth's remotest shores
E.g., among Our loved, low-German Boers,
Freely Our folk expectorate, and there
Our German bands inflame the balmy air;
Likewise again Our passionate bassoons
Tickle the niggers of the Cameroons;
Or others over whom Our Eagle flaps
In places not at present on the maps.
One more Imperial pint! your Kaiser drinks
To German intercourse with missing links!
Let loose the breathings of Our Royal Band,
We give hoch! hoch! Our glorious HINTERLAND!

[Kaiserliche Kapelle plays: O Hinterland! mein Hinterland! (Air as before); during
which WILLIAM, KAISER, resumes his throne.]

'The Spacious Times'
[On Drake's return from his filibustering expedition of 1580 the Queen went on
board his ship at Deptford, and after partaking of a banquet conferred on him
the honour of knighthood, at the same time declaring herself mightily pleased
with all that he had done.]

I wish that I had flourished then,
When ruffs and raids were in the fashion,
When Shakespeare's art and Raleigh's pen
Encouraged patriotic passion;
For though I draw my happy breath
Beneath a Queen as good and gracious,
The times of Great Elizabeth
Were more conveniently spacious.

Large-hearted age of cakes and ale!
When, undeterred by nice conditions,
Good Master Drake would lightly sail
On little privateer commissions;
Careering round with sword and flame
And no pretence of polished manners,

He planted out in England's name
A most refreshing lot of banners.

Blest era, when the reckless tar,
Elated by a sense of duty,
Feared not to face his country's Bar
But freely helped himself to booty;
Returning home with bulging hold
The Queen would meet him, much excited,
Pronounce him worth his weight in gold
And promptly have the hero knighted.

No Extra Special, piping hot,
Broke out in unexpected Pyrrhics;
No Poet Laureate on the spot
Composed apologetic lyrics;
Transpiring slowly by-and-by,
The act was voted one of loyalty;
The nation winked the other eye,
And pocketed the usual royalty.

Ere Reuter yet had found his range,
These trifles done across the ocean
Produced upon the Stock Exchange
No preternatural emotion;
Not yet the Kaiserlich I AM
Made wingéd words and then repented;
He wrote as yet no telegram,
Nor was, in fact, himself invented.

No Justice Hawkins gauged the fault
Of irresponsible incursions;
The early Hawkins, gallant salt,
Knew well the charm of such diversions;
Men never saw that moving sight
When legal luminaries muster,
And very solemnly indict
A well-conducted filibuster.

No Member had the hardy nerve
To criticise our depredations
As unadapted to preserve
The perfect comity of nations;
No High Commissioner would doubt
If brigandage was quite judicial;
Indeed we mostly did without
This rather eminent Official.

No Ministry would care a rap
For theoretic arbitration;
They simply modified the map
To meet the latest annexation;

And so without appeal to law,
Or other needless waste of tissue,
The Lion, where he put his paw,
Remained and propagated issue.

To-day we wax exceeding fat
On lands our roving fathers raided;
And blush with holy horror at
Their lawless sons who do as they did;
No doubt the age improves a lot,
It grows more honest, more veracious;
But, as I said, the times are not
Quite so conveniently spacious.

The Avengers

Not only that your cause is just and right
This much was never doubted; war or play,
We go with clean hands into any fight;
That is our English way;

Not this high thought alone shall brace your thews
To trample under heel those Vandal hordes
Who laugh when blood of mother and babe imbrues
Their damnèd craven swords.

But here must be hot passion, white of flame,
Pure hate of this unutterable wrong,
Sheer wrath for Christendom so sunk in shame,
To make you trebly strong.

These smoking hearths of fair and peaceful lands,
This reeking trail of deeds abhorred of Hell,
They cry aloud for vengeance at your hands,
Ruthless and swift and fell.

Strike, then - and spare not - for the innocent dead
Who lie there, stark beneath the weeping skies,
As though you saw your dearest in their stead
Butchered before your eyes.

And though the guiltless pay for others' guilt
Who preached these brute ideals in camp and Court;
Though lives of brave and gentle foes be spilt,
That loathe this coward sport;

On each, without distinction, worst or best
Fouled by a nation's crime, one doom must fall;
Be you its instrument, and leave the rest
To God, the Judge of all.

Let it be said of you, when sounds at length

Over the final field the victor's strain:
'They struck at infamy with all their strength,
And earth is clean again!'

Pro Patria

England, in this great fight to which you go
Because, where Honour calls you, go you must,
Be glad, whatever comes, at least to know
You have your quarrel just.

Peace was your care; before the nations' bar
Her cause you pleaded and her ends you sought;
But not for her sake, being what you are,
Could you be bribed and bought.

Others may spurn the pledge of land to land,
May with the brute sword stain a gallant past;
But by the seal to which
you
set your hand,
Thank God, you still stand fast!

Forth, then, to front that peril of the deep
With smiling lips and in your eyes the light,
Steadfast and confident, of those who keep
Their storied 'scutcheon bright.

And we, whose burden is to watch and wait,
High-hearted ever, strong in faith and prayer,
We ask what offering we may consecrate,
What humble service share.

To steel our souls against the lust of ease;
To bear in silence though our hearts may bleed;
To spend ourselves, and never count the cost,
For others' greater need;

To go our quiet ways, subdued and sane;
To hush all vulgar clamour of the street;
With level calm to face alike the strain
Of triumph or defeat;

This be our part, for so we serve you best,
So best confirm their prowess and their pride,
Your warrior sons, to whom in this high test
Our fortunes we confide.

Dies Irae
To the German Kaiser

Amazing Monarch! who at various times,
Posing as Europe's self-appointed saviour,
Afforded copy for our ribald rhymes
By your behaviour;

We nursed no malice; nay, we thanked you much
Because your head-piece, swollen like a tumour,
Lent to a dullish world the needed touch
Of saving humour.

What with your wardrobes stuffed with warrior gear,
Your gander-step parades, your prancing Prussians,
Your menaces that shocked the deafened sphere
With rude concussions;

Your fist that turned the pinkest rivals pale
Alike with sceptre, chisel, pen or palette,
And could at any moment, gloved in mail,
Smite like a mallet;

Master of all the Arts, and, what was more,
Lord of the limelight blaze that let us know it
You seemed a gift designed on purpose for
The flippant poet.

Time passed and put to these old jests an end;
Into our open hearts you found admission,
Ate of our bread and pledged us like a friend
Above suspicion.

You shared our griefs with seeming-gentle eyes;
You moved among us cousinly entreated;
Still hiding, under that fair outward guise,
A heart that cheated.

And now the mask is down, and forth you stand
Known for a King whose word is no great matter,
A traitor proved, for every honest hand
To strike and shatter.

This was the 'Day' foretold by yours and you
In whispers here, and there with beery clamours
You and your rat-hole spies and blustering crew
Of loud Potsdamers.

And lo, there dawns another, swift and stern,
When on the wheels of wrath, by Justice' token,
Breaker of God's own Peace, you shall in turn
Yourself be broken.

For The Red Cross

Ye that have gentle hearts and fain
To succour men in need,
There is no voice could ask in vain
With such a cause to plead
The cause of those that in your care,
Who know the debt to honour due,
Confide the wounds they proudly wear,
The wounds they took for you.

And yonder where the battle's waves
Broke yesterday o'erhead,
Where now the swift and shallow graves
Cover our English dead,
Think how your sisters play their part,
Who serve as in a holy shrine,
Tender of hand and brave of heart,
Under the Red Cross Sign.

Ah, by that symbol, worshipped still,
Of life-blood sacrificed,
That lonely Cross on Calvary's hill
Red with the wounds of Christ;
By that free gift to none denied,
Let Pity pierce you like a sword,
And love go out to open wide
The gate of life restored.

Probation: To A King's Recruit

Now is your time of trial, now
When into dusk the glamour pales
And the first glow of passion fails
That lit your eyes and flushed your brow
In that great moment when you made your vow.

The Vision fades; you scarce recall
The sudden swelling of the heart,
The swift resolve to have your part
In this the noblest quest of all
By which our word is given to stand or fall.

Your mother's pride, your comrades' praise
All that romance that seemed so fair
Grows dim, and you are left to bear
The prose of duty's sombre ways
And labour of the long unlovely days.

Yet here's the test to prove you kin
With those to whom we trust our fate,
Sober and stedfast, clean and straight,
In that stern school of discipline
Hardened to war against the foe within.

For only so, in England's sight,
By that ordeal's searching flame
Found worthy of your fathers' fame,
With all your spirit's armour bright
Can you go forth in her dear cause to fight.

Fashions For Men

There are who hanker for a touch of colour,
So to relieve their sombre air;
For me, I like my clothes to be much duller
Than what the nigger minstrels wear;
I hold by sable, drab and grey;
I do not wish to be a popinjay.

In vain my poor imagination grapples
With these new lines in fancy shades,
These purple evening coats with yellow lapels,
These vests composed in flowered brocades;
Nor can I think that noisy checks
Would help me to attract the other sex.

With gaudy schemes that rouse my solemn dander
I leave our frivolous youth to flirt;
A riband round my straw for choice, Leander;
A subtle nuance in my shirt;
For tie, the colours of my school
These are the limits of my austere rule.

But, when they'd have me swathe the clamorous tartan
In lieu of trousers round my waist,
Then they evoke the spirit of the Spartan
Inherent in my simple taste;
Inexorably I decline
To drape the kilt on any hips of mine.

It may be they will count me over-modest,
Deem me Victorian, dub me prude;
I may have early views, the very oddest,
On what is chaste and what is rude;
Yet am I certain that my leg
Would not look right beneath a filibeg.

I love the Scot as being truly British;
Golf (and the Union) makes us one;
Yet to my nature, which is far from skittish
And lacks his local sense of fun,
There is a something almost foreign
About his strange attachment to the sporran.

So, when a bargain-sale is held of chattels

Surviving from the recent War
Textiles and woollens, built for use in battles
And Scotland's there inquiring for
The kilt department, I shall not
Be found competing. She can have the lot.

T.M.G
Farewell, my CONSTANTINE! A guardian navy
Facilitates your exit on the blue;
For Greece has been this long while in the gravy
And he that put her there was plainly you;
'TINO MUST GO!' was writ for all to see,
Or, briefly, 'T.M.G.'

Whither, dear Sir, do you propose to sally?
To Switzerland's recuperative air,
To sip condensed milk in a private chalet
Or pluck the lissom chamois from his lair,
Or on the summit of a neutral Alp
Recline your crownless scalp?

Or did you ask from him you love so dearly
A royal haven fenced from rude alarms,
Even though WILLIAM should reserve you merely
A bedroom at 'The Hohenzollern Arms,'
Having for poor relations on the loose
No sort of further use?

Beware! I gather he might clasp his TINO
Only too warmly to his heaving chest,
Saying, 'O how reward such merits? We know!
Thou shalt command an Army in the West!
Yes, thou shalt bear upon the British Front
The pick of all the brunt.'

Frankly, if I were you, I wouldn't chance it.
Fighting has never really been your forte;
Witness Larissa, and your rapid transit,
Chivied by slow foot-sloggers of the Porte;
Far better make for Denmark o'er the foam;
There is no place like home.

Try some ancestral palace, well-appointed;
For choice the one where Hamlet nursed his spite,
Who found the times had grown a bit disjointed
And he was not the man to put 'em right;
And there consult on that enchanted shore
The ghosts of Elsinore.

Thomas Of The Light Heart

Facing the guns, he jokes as well
As any Judge upon the Bench;
Between the crash of shell and shell
His laughter rings along the trench;
He seems immensely tickled by a
Projectile which he calls a 'Black Maria.'

He whistles down the day-long road,
And, when the chilly shadows fall
And heavier hangs the weary load,
Is he down-hearted? Not at all.
'T is then he takes a light and airy
View of the tedious route to Tipperary.

His songs are not exactly hymns;
He never learned them in the choir;
And yet they brace his dragging limbs
Although they miss the sacred fire;
Although his choice and cherished gems
Do not include 'The Watch upon the Thames.'

He takes to fighting as a game;
He does no talking, through his hat,
Of holy missions; all the same
He has his faith-be sure of that;
He'll not disgrace his sporting breed,
Nor play what isn't cricket. There's his creed.

The Wayside Calvary
Now with the full year Memory holds her tryst
Heavy with such a tale of bitter loss
As never Earth has suffered since the Christ
Hung for us on the Cross.

If God, O Kaiser, makes the vision plain:
Gives you on some lone Calvary to see
The Man of Sorrows Who endured the pain
And died to set us free

How will you face beneath its Crown of thorn
That Figure stark against the smoking skies,
The Arms outstretched, the Sacred Head forlorn
And those reproachful Eyes?

How dare confront the false quest with the true
Or think what gulfs between the ideals lie
Of Him Who died that men might live - and you
Who live that men may die.

Ah, turn your eyes away: He reads your heart;
Pass on and, having done your work abhorred,

Join hands with Judas in his place apart,
You who betrayed your Lord.

To Belgium In Exile

Land of the desolate, Mother of tears,
Weeping your beauty marred and torn,
Your children tossed upon the spears,
Your altars rent, your hearths forlorn,
Where Spring has no renewing spell,
And Love no language save a long Farewell!

Ah, precious tears, and each a pearl,
Whose price-for so in God we trust
Who saw them fall in that blind swirl
Of ravening flame and reeking dust-
The spoiler with his life shall pay,
When Justice at the last demands her Day.

O tried and proved, whose record stands
Lettered in blood too deep to fade,
Take courage! Never in our hands
Shall the avenging sword be stayed
Till you are healed of all your pain,
And come with Honour to your own again.

Tactless Tactics

Were I a burglar in the dock
With every chance of doing time,
With Justice sitting like a rock
To hear a record black with crime;
If my conviction seemed a cert,
Yet, by a show of late repentance,
I thought I might, with luck, avert
A simply crushing sentence;

I should adopt, by use of art,
A pensive air of new-born grace,
In hope to melt the Bench's heart
And mollify its awful face;
I should not go and run amok,
Nor in a fit of senseless fury
Punch the judicial nose or chuck
An inkpot at the jury.

So with the Hun: you might assume
He would exert his homely wits
To mitigate the heavy doom
That else would break him all to bits;
Yet he behaves as one possessed,
Rampaging like a bull of Bashan,

Which, as I think, is not the best
Means of conciliation.

For when the wild beast, held and bound,
Ceases to plunge and rave and snort,
The Bench, I hope, will pass some sound
Remarks on this contempt of court;
The plea for mercy, urged too late,
Should prove a negligible cipher,
And when the sentence seals his fate
He'll get at least a lifer.

The Uses Of Ocean

To people who allege that we
Incline to overrate the Sea
I answer, 'We do not;
Apart from being colored blue,
It has its uses not a few;
I cannot think what we should do
If ever 'the deep did rot."

Take ships, for instance. You will note
That, lacking stuff on which to float,
They could not get about;
Dreadnought and liner, smack and yawl,
And other types that you'll recall
They simply could not sail at all
If Ocean once gave out.

And see the trouble which it saves
To islands; but for all those waves
That made us what we are
But for their help so kindly lent,
Europe could march right through to Kent
And never need to circumvent
A single British tar.

Take fish, again. I have in mind
No better field that they could find
For exercise or sport;
How would the whale, I want to know,
The blubbery whale contrive to blow?
Where would your playful kipper go
If the supply ran short?

And hence we rank the Ocean high;
But there are privy reasons why
Its praise is on my lip:
I deem it, when my heart is set
On walking into something wet,

The nicest medium I have met
In which to take a dip.

To The Memory Of Field-Marshall Earl Roberts

He died, as soldiers die, amid the strife,
Mindful of England in his latest prayer;
God, of His love, would have so fair a life
Crowned with a death as fair.

He might not lead the battle as of old,
But, as of old, among his own he went,
Breathing a faith that never once grew cold,
A courage still unspent.

So was his end; and, in that hour, across
The face of War a wind of silence blew,
And bitterest foes paid tribute to the loss
Of a great heart and true.

But we who loved him, what have we to lay
For sign of worship on his warrior-bier?
What homage, could his lips but speak to-day,
Would he have held most dear?

Not grief, as for a life untimely reft;
Not vain regret for counsel given in vain;
Not pride of that high record he has left,
Peerless and pure of stain;

But service of our lives to keep her free,
The land he served; a pledge above his grave
To give her even such a gift as he,
The soul of loyalty, gave.

That oath we plight, as now the trumpets swell
His requiem, and the men-at-arms stand mute,
And through the mist the guns he loved so well
Thunder a last salute!

The Prophetic Present

By nature they abhor the light,
But here in this their latest tract
Your parrot Press by oversight
Has deviated into fact;
If not (at present) strictly true,
It shows a sound anticipation
Born of the fear that's father to
The allegation.

For, though the boasted 'line' of which

No trace occurs on German maps
Retains the semblance of a ditch,
It has some nasty yawning gaps;
It bulges here, it wobbles there,
It crumples up with broken hinges,
Keeping no sort of pattern where
Our Push impinges.

When the triumphant word went round
How that your god, disguised as man,
At victory's height was giving ground
According to a well-laid plan,
Here he arranged to draw the line
(As Siegfried's you were told to hymn it)
And plant Nil ultra for a sign
Meaning the limit.

And now 'There's no such thing,' they say;
Well, that implies prophetic sense;
And, if a British prophet may
Adopt their graphic present tense,
I would remark and so forestall
A truth they'll never dare to trench on:
There is no HINDENBURG at all,
Or none worth mention.

www.ingramcontent.com/pod-product-compliance
Lightning Source LLC
Chambersburg PA
CBHW060100050426
42448CB00011B/2550